STATES

INDIANA

A MyReportLinks.com Book

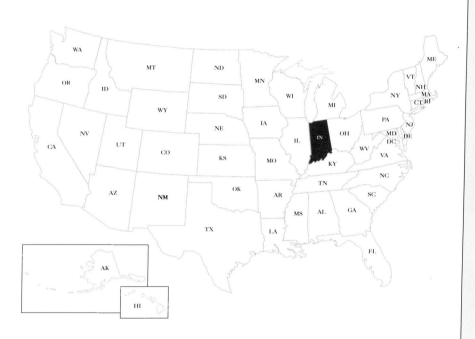

Ron Knapp

MyReportLinks.com Books

an imprint of
Enslow Publishers, Inc.
Box 398, 40 Industrial Road
Berkeley Heights, NJ 07922
USA

Back   Forward   Stop   Review   Home   Explore   Favorites   History

MyReportLinks.com Books, an imprint of Enslow Publishers, Inc. MyReportLinks is a trademark of Enslow Publishers, Inc.

Library of Congress Cataloging-in-Publication Data

Knapp, Ron.
  Indiana / Ron Knapp.
      p. cm. — (States)
  Summary: Discusses the land and climate, economy, government, and history of the state of Indiana. Includes Internet links to Web sites.
  Includes bibliographical references and index.
    ISBN 0-7660-5118-8
    1. Indiana—Juvenile literature. [1. Indiana.] I. Title. II. States
  (Series : Berkeley Heights, N.J.)
    F526.3 .K63 2003
    977.2—dc21
                                    2002152453

Printed in the United States of America

10 9 8 7 6 5 4 3 2 1

To Our Readers:
Through the purchase of this book, you and your library gain access to the Report Links that specifically back up this book.

The Publisher will provide access to the Report Links that back up this book and will keep these Report Links up to date on **www.myreportlinks.com** for three years from the book's first publication date.

We have done our best to make sure all Internet addresses in this book were active and appropriate when we went to press. However, the author and the Publisher have no control over, and assume no liability for, the material available on those Internet sites or on other Web sites they may link to.

The usage of the MyReportLinks.com Books Web site is subject to the terms and conditions stated on the Usage Policy Statement on **www.myreportlinks.com**.

In the future, a password may be required to access the Report Links that back up this book. The password is found on the bottom of page 4 of this book.

Any comments or suggestions can be sent by e-mail to comments@myreportlinks.com or to the address on the back cover.

Photo Credits: City of Indianapolis, Marion County, p. 39; © Corel Corporation, pp. 3, 10; Enslow Publishers, Inc., pp. 1, 19; Eugene V. Debs Foundation, p. 27; Fairmont Historical Museum, p. 31; Friends of Angel Mounds, Inc., p. 41; Indiana Basketball Hall of Fame, p. 14; Indiana Department of Commerce, pp. 12, 18, 21, 22, 36, 37, 43, 44; Indiana Native Plant and Wildflower Society, p. 23; IndyStar.com, p. 35; Library of Congress, p. 3 (Constitution); MyReportLinks.com Books, p. 4; Ryan White Foundation, p. 33; Student Advantage, Inc. and the University of Notre Dame, p. 29; The Digital Library Program and The Archives of Traditional Music at Indiana University, p. 17; The National Speleological Society, p. 20; U.S. Geological Survey, p. 25.

Cover Photo: AP/Wide World Photos.

Contents

Report Links 4

Indiana Facts 10

1   Crossroads of America 11

2   Land and Attractions 18

3   Interesting People 26

4   The Government, Economy,
    and Cities 36

5   History 41

    Chapter Notes 46

    Further Reading 47

    Index 48

MyReportLinks.com Books
Great Books, Great Links, Great for Research!

MyReportLinks.com Books present the information you need to learn about your report subject. In addition, they show you where to go on the Internet for more information. The pre-evaluated Report Links that back up this book are kept up to date on **www.myreportlinks.com**. With the purchase of a MyReportLinks.com Books title, you and your library gain access to the Report Links that specifically back up that book. The Report Links save hours of research time and link to dozens—even hundreds—of Web sites, source documents, and photos related to your report topic.

Please see "To Our Readers" on the Copyright page for important information about this book, the MyReportLinks.com Books Web site, and the Report Links that back up this book.

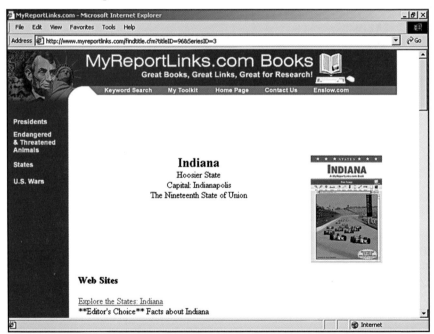

Access:

The Publisher will provide access to the Report Links that back up this book and will try to keep these Report Links up to date on our Web site for three years from the book's first publication date. Please enter **SIN2952** if asked for a password.

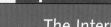
Report Links

The Internet sites described below can be accessed at
http://www.myreportlinks.com

▶ **Explore the States: Indiana**   *EDITOR'S CHOICE

America's Story from America's Library, a Library of Congress Web site,
provides facts about Indiana. You will also find other stories relating to
Indiana's culture and history.

Link to this Internet site from http://www.myreportlinks.com

▶ **Indiana Historical Society**   *EDITOR'S CHOICE

The Indiana Historical Society collects and shares information about
Indiana's heritage. View listings of exhibits and collections. Be sure to
look for the "Today in Indiana History" section for interesting facts.

Link to this Internet site from http://www.myreportlinks.com

▶ **Indiana Maps**   *EDITOR'S CHOICE

Perry-Castañeda Library holds an online collection of maps of Indiana.
Here you will find state maps, city maps, and maps of national parks,
monuments, and historic sites.

Link to this Internet site from http://www.myreportlinks.com

▶ **U.S. Census Bureau Quick Facts**   *EDITOR'S CHOICE

Get Indiana state and county quick facts from the U.S. Census Bureau.
See population, business, and geography information for the state, as
well as individual counties.

Link to this Internet site from http://www.myreportlinks.com

▶ **The official Web site of the City of Indianapolis
and Marion County, Indiana**   *EDITOR'S CHOICE

At the official Web site of the City of Indianapolis and Marion County
you will find information about government, community, business, and
visiting, as well as a kids section.

Link to this Internet site from http://www.myreportlinks.com

▶ **NETSTATE: Indiana**   *EDITOR'S CHOICE

Learn about the history of Indiana, and view its state symbols as well as
a list of famous "Hoosiers." Test your knowledge with the "State Quiz,"
and get interesting facts from the "Almanac."

Link to this Internet site from http://www.myreportlinks.com

Any comments? Contact us: **comments@myreportlinks.com**   5

Report Links

The Internet sites described below can be accessed at
http://www.myreportlinks.com

▶ **The American Presidency: William Henry Harrison**
An informative biography of America's ninth president, William Henry
Harrison. Read about the life of the president who served the shortest term in
history. Details include Harrison's early years, marriage, family, military career,
and presidency.

Link to this Internet site from http://www.myreportlinks.com

▶ **Angel Mounds State Historical Site**
Explore what was once the largest town in Indiana, Angel Mounds. The Angel
Mounds State Historical Site provides a history of the site, events, exhibits,
and a kids section.

Link to this Internet site from http://www.myreportlinks.com

▶ **Battle of Tippecanoe**
This Web site tells the story of the Battle of Tippecanoe and how the governor
of the Indiana Territory, William Henry Harrison, led his army into battle.

Link to this Internet site from http://www.myreportlinks.com

▶ **Canal Society of Indiana**
The Canal Society of Indiana was founded in 1982 to educate and focus
attention on the preservation and restoration of canal beds and structural
remains. Learn about the history of the canals, view photos, and see what is
planned for the future.

Link to this Internet site from http://www.myreportlinks.com

▶ **County History Preservation Society: Covered Bridges**
Indiana is known as the "Covered Bridge Capital." View photos, and learn
about these historic covered bridges. Each bridge is listed by county location.

Link to this Internet site from http://www.myreportlinks.com

▶ **Henry Ford Museum and Greenfield Village: The Wright Brothers**
Read about the lives of the famous Wright brothers. Wilbur Wright was born
in Indiana. What inspired their interest in flight? Learn about this as well as
the world's first airplane. Photos of the airplane and more are available.

Link to this Internet site from http://www.myreportlinks.com

Report Links

The Internet sites described below can be accessed at
http://www.myreportlinks.com

▶ **Indiana Basketball Hall Fame**

Here is where athletes such as John Wooden and Larry Bird are
honored. Learn how players qualify for the Indiana Basketball Hall
Fame on this searchable site. Also read news and biographies on
Indiana basketball's most celebrated athletes.

Link to this Internet site from http://www.myreportlinks.com

▶ **Indiana Department of Natural Resources**

Here you will find information about Indiana's natural resources.
Learn about state parks, endangered species, and hunting and fishing.
You can also access other bureaus within the department from this site.

Link to this Internet site from http://www.myreportlinks.com

▶ **Indiana Historic Architecture**

The Indiana Historic Architecture Home Page is devoted to the
appreciation, restoration, and preservation of Indiana landmarks. Learn
how you can get involved in historic architecture preservation, and
view photos of historic Indiana landmarks.

Link to this Internet site from http://www.myreportlinks.com

▶ **Indiana History**

Find information about the history of Indiana, including ethnic
history, the Civil War, and historic events. You will also find facts about
American Indians in Indiana, maps, and a historical photo archive.

Link to this Internet site from http://www.myreportlinks.com

▶ **Indiana Karst Conservancy**

This Web site will tell you what a karst is. You can view photos of caves
and sinkholes and read about the topography of Indiana.

Link to this Internet site from http://www.myreportlinks.com

▶ **Indiana Native Plant and Wildflower Society**

The Indiana Native Plant and Wildflower Society promotes the
preservation of plants and wildflowers native to Indiana. Learn how to
incorporate these native plants into landscaping, and see what you can
do to help in the fight against invasive plants.

Link to this Internet site from http://www.myreportlinks.com

 The Internet sites described below can be accessed at
http://www.myreportlinks.com

▶**Indiana State Fact Sheet**
This fact sheet presents vital data such as population and employment rates in Indiana. You will also find information about the highest ranking counties for commodities, exports, and retail sales. Other state information is available as well.

Link to this Internet site from http://www.myreportlinks.com

▶**Indiana War Memorials**
The Indiana War Memorial Web site provides access to information about the Civil War, World War II, and much more. Take a virtual tour of the Civil War Museum, and view images of their battle flag collection.

Link to this Internet site from http://www.myreportlinks.com

▶**Indiana Woodlands Information**
At the Woodlands Steward home page you can learn about conservation efforts and the forest industry. You can also learn about different trees by visiting the "Tree Identification Section."

Link to this Internet site from http://www.myreportlinks.com

▶**James Dean Foundation: James Dean Artifacts**
James Dean was born in Marion County, Indiana, on February 8, 1931. At this Web site you will find a brief history of his life and many historical photographs.

Link to this Internet site from http://www.myreportlinks.com

▶**Kurt Vonnegut**
Kurt Vonnegut was born in Indianapolis, Indiana. Here you will find a brief overview of his life and how it has influenced many of his novels.

Link to this Internet site from http://www.myreportlinks.com

▶**Monroe County Public Library: Indiana Room**
The Indiana Room provides links to information about Indiana's history, facts, and state emblems. You can also read interesting theories about the origin of the state's nickname.

Link to this Internet site from http://www.myreportlinks.com

Report Links

The Internet sites described below can be accessed at
http://www.myreportlinks.com

▶ **Motor Sports Hall of Fame: Ray Harroun**
In the year 2000, Ray Harroun was inducted into the Motor Sports
Hall of Fame of America. He was the winner of the first ever
Indianapolis 500.

Link to this Internet site from http://www.myreportlinks.com

▶ **Official Site of the Eugene V. Debs Foundation**
Here you can explore the life of Eugene V. Debs. Learn how he ran for
president fives time as the Socialist Party candidate. You will also find
many photographs, and you can take a virtual tour of his home.

Link to this Internet site from http://www.myreportlinks.com

▶ **The Ports of Indiana**
Learn about the ports of Indiana. See where they are located and
how they relate to Indiana's economy. Read about actual companies
that use the ports to do business and what type of products and
services they sell.

Link to this Internet site from http://www.myreportlinks.com

▶ **Stats Indiana**
Find statistics about Indiana, including information from Census 2000,
the economy, the workforce, and population.

Link to this Internet site from http://www.myreportlinks.com

▶ **USGS: Butterflies of Indiana**
By clicking on Indiana on the map, you will find a list of butterflies in
that state. For instance, you can learn about the Swallowtails, Whites
and Sulphurs, Metalmarks, and many others.

Link to this Internet site from http://www.myreportlinks.com

▶ **VisitIndiana: Sports**
Hoosier's love their sports! Find all of the major and professional league
teams here. From basketball to hockey, both male and female teams are
featured. The Indianapolis Motor Speedway features photos and
statistics from the Indy 500.

Link to this Internet site from http://www.myreportlinks.com

Indiana Facts

Capital
Indianapolis

Counties
92

Gained Statehood
December 11, 1816, the nineteenth state

Population
6,080,485*

Bird
Cardinal

Tree
Tulip Tree

Flower
Peony

Stone
Limestone

River
Wabash River

Poem
"Indiana" (by Arthur Franklin Mapes)

Song
"On the Banks of the Wabash, Far Away" (words and music by Paul Dresser)

Motto
The Crossroads of America

Nickname
Hoosier State

Flag
A blue flag with a gold torch in the middle. Around the torch is an outer circle of thirteen gold stars representing the thirteen original states. In a half circle under the torch are five gold stars representing the states admitted to the union prior to Indiana. A larger gold star representing the state of Indiana is placed above the torch. Between the larger star and the outer circle of stars is the word "Indiana" written in a half circle. Rays radiate from the torch to the three stars in the outer circle on both sides of the Indiana star.[1]

Population reflects the 2000 census.

Chapter 1

Crossroads of America

Size can be deceiving. Take Indiana, for example. Except for Hawaii, it is the smallest state west of the Appalachian Mountains. Its 35,870 square miles of land area is less than one-sixteenth the size of Alaska.

Despite its size, Indiana has 6,085,485 people. That makes it the fourteenth most populous state. Its motto is "The Crossroads of America." More highways cross Indiana than any other state.

Indiana, of course, is known for much more than just roads. Its athletes and sports teams have thrilled fans for generations.

▶ Speed on the Track

The world-famous Indianapolis Motor Speedway has 250,000 permanent seats, more than any other facility in the world. Many people feel Memorial Day would not be the same without the Indianapolis 500.

Every seat is taken as the race cars whirl around the two-and-a-half-mile track at speeds greater than 200 miles per hour. Races have been held there ever since Carl Fisher came up with the idea for a long track in the early 1900s. Why, he asked, do tracks have to be limited to just a mile? Would it not be more interesting to have a longer course?

In 1909, the first race was held at the Speedway. Two years later came the first Indianapolis 500 race. Ray Harroun was the winner, averaging 74.6 miles per hour, an incredible speed in those days.

▲ Home to the Indianapolis 500, the Indianapolis Motor Speedway is a major tourist attraction in Indiana.

Through the years, the crowds have grown, and the speeds have increased. The closest and one of the most exciting finishes came in 1992. After 500 miles and 200 laps, Al Unser, Jr., beat Scott Goodyear by just .043 seconds.

▶ Football Thrills

The University of Notre Dame is not a big place. Located in South Bend, Indiana, it has only about ten thousand students. A hundred years ago when it was just a college, it was much smaller. It was a Catholic school built to educate the sons of Irish immigrants. Hardly anybody noticed little Notre Dame until the student athletes there began to excel at what was then the new sport of football.

When the powerful Army team battled the Notre Dame Fighting Irish in 1913, it was not supposed to be much of a game. After Notre Dame took a stunning 35–13 victory, fans began to take notice. One of the stars in that upset was a receiver named Knute Rockne. Five years later, he was the team's coach.

Rockne made Notre Dame into a powerhouse. Along the way, he became one of the country's most popular personalities. Ever since then, the Fighting Irish have been one of the nation's most powerful and successful teams. Notre Dame has won twelve national football championships, more than any other team.

▶ Indiana's Sport

Auto racing and football may be popular in Indiana, but if you want to find out the state's favorite sport, look at the driveways and playgrounds. You will see thousands of basketball hoops. Everybody in the state, it seems, has a basket.

The Hoosiers of Indiana University have been crowned NCAA champions five times. In 2002, Indiana came just one game short of taking the title again.

John Wooden, the most successful college basketball coach ever, led the University of California at Los Angeles (UCLA) to ten NCAA titles. As a teenager, he played on the Martinsville High School team that won the 1927 Indiana state championship. Then, he was an All-American at Purdue, a college in West Lafayette, Indiana.

It is not just the college athletes who excel at the sport. The Indiana Pacers were one of the best teams in the professional National Basketball Association's (NBA) Eastern Conference during the 1990s. One of the sport's greatest

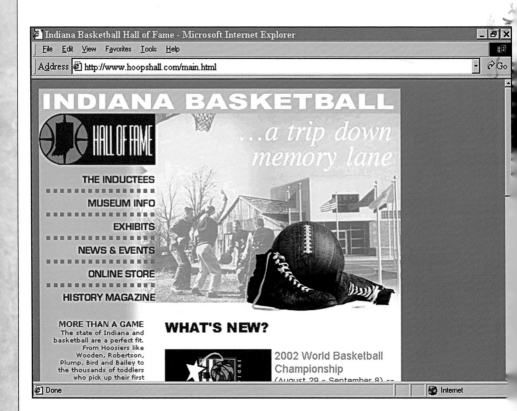

INDIANA BASKETBALL

HALL OF FAME

...a trip down memory lane

THE INDUCTEES

MUSEUM INFO

EXHIBITS

NEWS & EVENTS

ONLINE STORE

HISTORY MAGAZINE

MORE THAN A GAME
The state of Indiana and basketball are a perfect fit. From Hoosiers like Wooden, Robertson, Plump, Bird and Bailey to the thousands of toddlers who pick up their first

WHAT'S NEW?

2002 World Basketball Championship
(August 29 – September 8) --

Done   Internet

▲ *Basketball is a huge part of Indiana's culture. Indiana University has boasted great talent such as Isiah Thomas, while the Indiana Pacers have featured superstars like Reggie Miller and Jermaine O'Neal.*

stars was Larry Bird, from French Lick, Indiana, who led the Boston Celtics to three NBA titles.

▶ The Milan Miracle

A late winter tradition in Indiana is the state high school championship basketball tournament. Until recently, all the schools, despite their size, competed in the same bracket.

In 1954, the Milan Indians, a tiny school with just fifty students in its senior class, battled all the way to the championship game. They faced mighty Muncie Central, a much bigger school—and the defending state champions.

Halfway through the fourth quarter, the teams, incredibly enough, were tied, 30–30. Coach Marvin Wood of Milan had an unusual strategy. He told his player Bobby Plump to take the ball and stall for a final shot.

So Plump started stalling. For four minutes he dribbled around the court. The Muncie players chased him but could not get the ball. Finally, as time was about to run out, Plump heaved a jump shot toward the basket. It was good. Tiny Milan won the championship, 32–30. Years later, *Hoosiers*, a movie based on Milan's improbable victory, became a big hit.

▶ The Poet, the Authors, and the Composers

Of course there is lots more to Indiana than just roads, exciting sports, and great athletes. The state has also produced an interesting variety of creative individuals.

James Whitcomb Riley was born in Greenfield, Indiana, in 1849. While supporting himself as a sign painter, he began contributing poems to the *Indianapolis Journal*. His most popular works were not written in standard English. Instead he made his poems reflect the way Indiana's common people spoke. Two of his most popular works were "Out to Old Aunt Mary's" and "When the Frost Is on the Punkin." By the time of his death in 1916, Riley was known throughout the country as the "Hoosier Poet."

Ernie Pyle, born near Dana, Indiana, left college to become a reporter for the *LaPorte Herald-Argus*. During World War II, he was a correspondent covering battle action in Europe, Africa, and the Pacific Ocean. Pyle did not just write about the movements of troops and statistics. He concentrated on telling the stories of individual

soldiers. Two book-length collections of his articles, *Here Is Your War* and *Brave Men*, were best-sellers. Late in the war, Pyle was killed when he accompanied American servicemen on their mission against the Japanese on the island of le Shima, a few miles northwest of Okinawa.

Jessamyn West, an Indiana author, belonged to the Quaker religion. Her beliefs are an important part of her novels. *The Friendly Persuasion*, published in 1945, was her most important book. In it she wrote about the quiet life of Quakers in the nineteenth century.

Born in Indianapolis, Kurt Vonnegut, Jr., became one of the most famous writers of the second half of the twentieth century. During World War II, Vonnegut, Jr., was an American prisoner of war during the bombing of Dresden, Germany. That experience inspired him to write *Slaughterhouse-Five*, a shocking antiwar novel.

In that and other books, Vonnegut used science fiction and the bizarre adventures of his characters to paint a sad picture of how human beings hurt each other. His other novels include *Cat's Cradle* and *Breakfast of Champions*.

If not for his asthma, Jim Davis probably would have become a farmer. After his birth, in 1945, he lived on his family's cow farm near Marion, Indiana. Unfortunately, his health problems kept him inside most of the time. Interestingly, the Davis farm was home to as many as twenty-five stray cats. Davis spent much of his time inside doodling and drawing them.

In 1978, he began drawing a comic strip about a cat named after his grandfather, James Garfield Davis. Since then, the adventures of Garfield the cat have become one of the most popular comic strips in the world. Garfield was only the third strip to be printed in two thousand newspapers each day.[1]

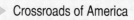

Cole Porter, a native of Peru, Indiana, began writing songs when he was still a child. His first big hit, "Bulldog, Bulldog," the Yale fight song, came in 1913. Porter's best-known song is probably "I've Got You Under My Skin."

Hoagy Carmichael was a native of Bloomington, Indiana. He wrote "Star Dust," a soft, beautiful tune, in 1927. It has become one of the world's most performed and recorded songs. Carmichael continued to write music as he starred in movies and hosted television and radio programs.

Each of these people, and others, have contributed to the unique history of the state of Indiana and were influenced by growing up in the Midwest.

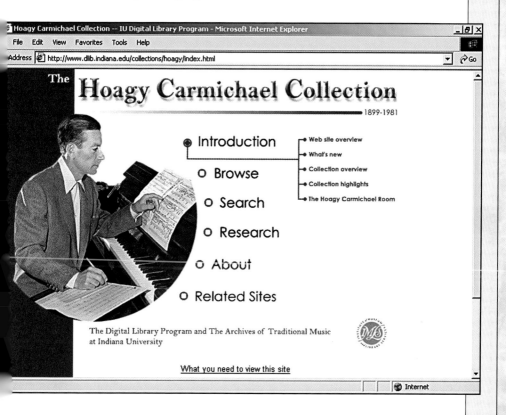

▲ Hoagy Carmichael's song "Star Dust" is one of the most widely recognized tunes in music history.

17

Chapter 2

Land and Attractions

Glaciers sculpted Indiana into the land it is today. For thousands of years, the giant oceans of ice scraped back and forth across the American Midwest. As a result, the land under them was flattened. The last of the glaciers melted about ten thousand years ago.

The only good-sized hills in the state are in the south, the only region not covered by the last glaciers. The northern two thirds of the state is remarkably flat.

Geologists have divided Indiana into three regions. The Great Lakes Plains is the northern area that borders

▲ These hills in Madison, Indiana, are typical of the southern part of the state.

Lake Michigan

MICHIGAN

Michigan City ●
Whiting ●   ● South Bend
● ● Burns Harbor
Gary   ● Nappanee

GREAT LAKES PLAINS

Fort Wayne ●

N

● Peru

Wabash River

West Lafayette ● Battle Ground

● Marion

● Portland

Kokomo ●

ILLINOIS

TILL PLAINS

● Muncie

Cicero ●

OHIO

● Dana   New Castle ●

Indianapolis ✪   ● Greenfield

● Mooresville

● Terre Haute   ● Martinsville

Bloomington ●   Monroe Lake   ● Milan

Ohio River

Madison ●   Ohio River

● Vincennes

● French Lick

SOUTHERN HILLS AND LOWLANDS

● Leavenworth
● Corydon

● Evansville

KENTUCKY

🔺 A map of Indiana.

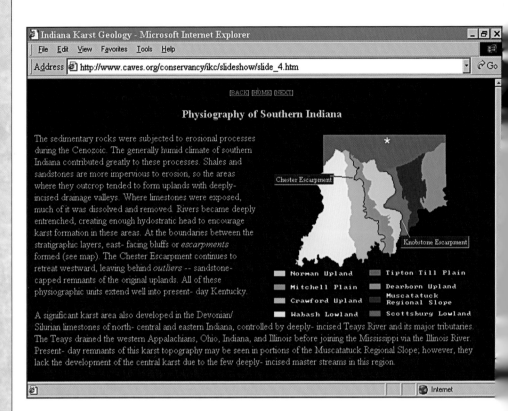

[BACK] [HOME] [NEXT]

Physiography of Southern Indiana

The sedimentary rocks were subjected to erosional processes during the Cenozoic. The generally humid climate of southern Indiana contributed greatly to these processes. Shales and sandstones are more impervious to erosion, so the areas where they outcrop tended to form uplands with deeply-incised drainage valleys. Where limestones were exposed, much of it was dissolved and removed. Rivers became deeply entrenched, creating enough hydostratic head to encourage karst formation in these areas. At the boundaries between the stratigraphic layers, east- facing bluffs or *escarpments* formed (see map). The Chester Escarpment continues to retreat westward, leaving behind *outliers* -- sandstone-capped remnants of the original uplands. All of these physiographic units extend well into present- day Kentucky.

Chester Escarpment

Knobstone Escarpment

- Norman Upland
- Mitchell Plain
- Crawford Upland
- Wabash Lowland
- Tipton Till Plain
- Dearborn Upland
- Muscatatuck Regional Slope
- Scottsburg Lowland

A significant karst area also developed in the Devonian/ Silurian limestones of north- central and eastern Indiana, controlled by deeply- incised Teays River and its major tributaries. The Teays drained the western Appalachians, Ohio, Indiana, and Illinois before joining the Mississippi via the Illinois River. Present- day remnants of this karst topography may be seen in portions of the Muscatatuck Regional Slope; however, they lack the development of the central karst due to the few deeply- incised master streams in this region.

▲ Over time, Indiana's geography eroded to such a degree that valleys were formed.

Michigan. It is a fertile, moist region with many lakes and rivers. Along the tiny strip on the coast of Lake Michigan are beautiful, giant sand dunes.

The central part of the state is covered by the Till Plains. It has Indiana's most fertile soil. A few small hills break up the long stretches of flat land.

The last region is known, appropriately, as the Southern Hills and Lowlands. Many of its steepest hills are in long rows. Millions of years ago, this area was covered by an ocean. Over the centuries, the ancient bones of the sea creatures that lived here have hardened into limestone.

Underground rivers have slowly, but steadily, carved caves in the limestone.

In recent years, that rock has been used in the construction of many of the United States' most important buildings. The Empire State Building and the Pentagon were both built with Indiana limestone.

The Climate

Indiana has cool winters and warm summers. As you travel south, of course, temperatures tend to be warmer.

Lake Michigan has a major effect on the state's weather. Since the water is warmer than the surrounding land during the winter, it helps raise the temperature in areas near the shore. Moisture over the lake can turn to snow when it blows over land. That is why the coastal areas get much more snow than the rest of the state.

▲ Lake Michigan is the third largest of the Great Lakes as well as the only one to lie entirely within the boundaries of the United States. It is the largest body of freshwater in the country.

▷ Interesting Sites

Visitors who climb the northern dunes between Gary and Michigan City are treated to a beautiful view at the top. Acres of brilliant white sand stretch down to the bright blue of Lake Michigan.

Indiana Dunes National Lakeshore features long beaches and tall, sloping dunes. Visitors can swim, boat, hike, and picnic. Besides the sand and water, there are many interesting plants and animals.

The people of Indiana are proud that Abraham Lincoln grew up in their state. He moved here with his family when he was seven. The Lincolns' original log cabin is on display at the Lincoln Boyhood National Memorial in Lincoln City. It is also the site of the grave of his

▲ *Lincoln's Boyhood National Memorial preserves the log cabin President Abraham Lincoln lived in for fourteen years after he moved to Indiana in 1816.*

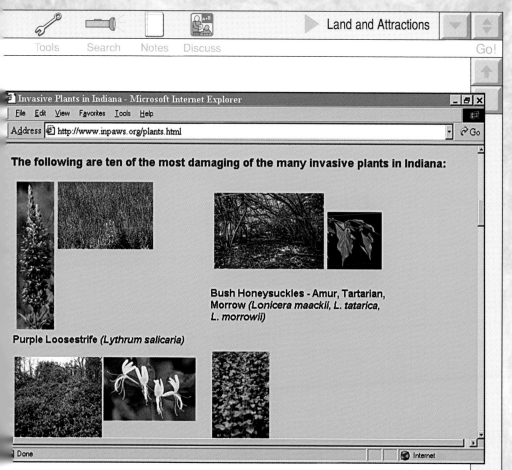

The following are ten of the most damaging of the many invasive plants in Indiana:

Bush Honeysuckles - Amur, Tartarian, Morrow (Lonicera maackii, L. tatarica, L. morrowii)

Purple Loosestrife (Lythrum salicaria)

▲ *The purple loosestrife and bush honeysuckles are two of about thirty-seven invasive plants found in Indiana. This means that they grow rapidly to cover an entire area, often eliminating other plants necessary to sustain local wildlife.*

mother, Nancy Hanks Lincoln. A working farm features actors in costume playing the part of the original settlers.

William Henry Harrison would most likely never have become president if he had not won the Battle of Tippecanoe. The battle, in which he defeated a coalition led by Chief Tecumseh of the Shawnee tribe, made him a national hero. Today there are artifacts and displays at the Tippecanoe Battlefield and Museum in Battle Ground, near Lafayette, Indiana.

The William Henry Harrison Home still stands in Vincennes. It was probably the first brick building in the state. Harrison lived there when he served as the territory's first governor.

Costumed soldiers are featured at Historic Fort Wayne, a reconstruction of an American army fort. Chief Little Turtle and General "Mad" Anthony Wayne are remembered by artifacts and displays.

Probably the best spot to learn about the lifestyle of the Amish religion is to visit Amish Acres, near Nappanee. The barn there is more than one hundred years old. Since it is still a working farm, apple cider, molasses, and maple syrup are produced there. Visitors can enjoy Amish cooking at local restaurants and purchase traditional crafts like candles, quilts, and rugs.

On days when races are not being run, the Indianapolis Motor Speedway is still a popular spot for tourists. They can examine vintage cars, then ride over the track itself in a small bus. Visitors may be surprised by what they find in the Speedway's infield. Four holes of an eighteen-hole golf course are surrounded by the track. The rest of the Brickyard Crossing course is located outside the stands.

Near Leavenworth, Indiana's limestone caves can be explored at Wyandotte Cave. There are more than thirty-five miles of caverns on five different levels.

Thousands of visitors come to Indiana each year to see the state's covered bridges. The first ones were built in the 1830s when the National Road was being constructed across the state. Since the bridges were made of wood, the builders covered them with roofs to protect them from rain and snow. This helped them to last longer.

During the nineteenth century, hundreds of covered bridges were built. By 1930, there were 202 of the bridges

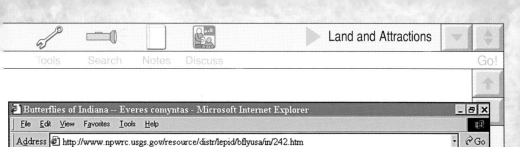

Eastern Tailed-Blue

⚠ *The eastern tailed-blue butterfly is a native of Indiana. They are commonly found in open, sunny areas.*

left in the state. Since then, that number has been cut in half. Many gradually weathered away or were simply replaced with modern structures. With new materials like steel and asphalt, it is no longer necessary to build wooden bridges. Those covered bridges that remain today have been restored and repaired.

Chapter 3

Interesting People

Indiana has been home to more than its share of fascinating personalities. They have not all lived exemplary lives. Some of them have even gotten in serious trouble. Still, as they pushed the boundaries in their chosen careers—from politics to sports to entertainment—they captured the attention of the nation.

▶ The Harrisons

Up to this time, William Henry Harrison and Benjamin Harrison are the only grandfather and grandson to both become president of the United States.

William Henry was the governor of the Indiana Territory for a dozen years. He led the troops who defeated a large force of American Indians at the Battle of Tippecanoe in 1811. William Henry Harrison was only president for a month. He died soon after being inaugurated in 1841.

Benjamin Harrison was born at his grandfather's home in Ohio. When he was a young lawyer, he moved to Indiana. During the Civil War, he was a brigadier general. Because he was just 5 feet 6 inches tall his soldiers nicknamed him "Little Ben."

After serving in the U.S. Senate, Benjamin defeated President Grover Cleveland in the election of 1888. Four years later, Cleveland turned the tables by beating him.

▶ Eugene V. Debs

Eugene V. Debs ran for president five times—once while he was in prison. He was born in Terre Haute in 1855 and went to work for a railroad company when he was only fifteen years old. Debs did not feel working people were treated fairly by the companies or by the government. The solution, he believed, was for the workers to join together in unions.

He eventually formed the American Railway Union. One of his strongest weapons was a strike, when his members refused to work until conditions and wages improved.

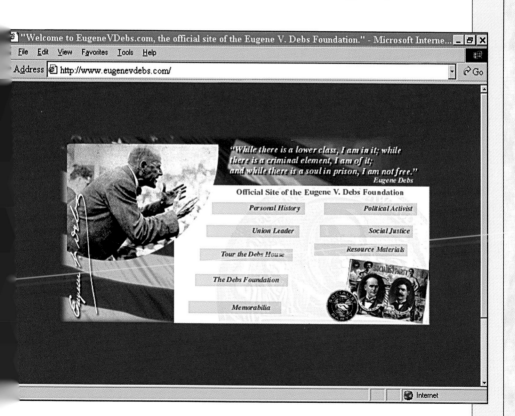

"Welcome to EugeneVDebs.com, the official site of the Eugene V. Debs Foundation." - Microsoft Interne...

File   Edit   View   Favorites   Tools   Help

Address http://www.eugenevdebs.com/

"While there is a lower class, I am in it; while there is a criminal element, I am of it; and while there is a soul in prison, I am not free."
Eugene Debs

Official Site of the Eugene V. Debs Foundation

Personal History	Political Activist
Union Leader	Social Justice
Tour the Debs House	Resource Materials
The Debs Foundation	
Memorabilia	

▲ Eugene V. Debs was a socialist union leader and politician. He spoke out in support of women's rights and the working class.

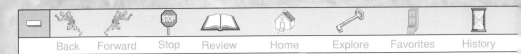

When the government ordered the union to end a strike in 1894, Debs refused. For that offense, he served six months in prison.[1]

While imprisoned, he became a supporter of socialism, a system of government in which the workers own and control the factories and businesses where they work. Debs's impassioned speeches made him a national figure. He was the Socialist Party's candidate for president in 1900, 1904, 1908, 1912, and 1920.

Debs condemned American involvement in World War I. He believed the country should concentrate on improving the lives of its people instead of fighting a foreign war. He was again arrested and convicted, this time under the Espionage Law. Even though he was in prison the last time he ran for president, he still received roughly 915,000 votes.

▶ Knute Rockne

How many little boys born in Norway grow up to become one of the most famous football coaches in history? Only one so far—Knute Rockne.

His family moved to the United States when he was five. After high school, he studied chemistry at the University of Notre Dame. While he was there, he tried out a new sport—football.

With Rockne as a receiver, Notre Dame became the first team to depend on passing, instead of running, to move the ball. Shortly after graduating in 1914, he became an assistant coach at the school and was named head coach in 1918. Soon the Fighting Irish were one of the most powerful football teams in the nation. Relying on the pass and shifting people around just before the ball was snapped, Rockne's teams were almost unbeatable.

NOTRE DAME FIGHTING IRISH, The Official Athletic Site, Football - Microsoft Internet Explorer

File   Edit   View   Favorites   Tools   Help

Address   http://und.ocsn.com/sports/m-footbl/nd-m-footbl-body.html

OFFICIAL ATHLETIC SITE

NOTRE DAME

Tickets | Schedules | Online Store | Camps | Links | Audio/Video | Travel | Site Map

FOOTBALL   CHOOSE SPORT »»»   MEN'S SPORTS   WOMEN'S SPORTS

> ROSTER
> SCHEDULE
> NEWS
> ARCHIVES

> On Campus
> Compliance
> Facilities
> Traditions
> In the News
> Game Promotions
> Hospitality
> Corporate Sponsors
> Monogram Club
> Student Development
> Kids Club
> General Releases

TOP STORIES

AP   11/26/02

Coach Willingham Press Conference Transcript

Notre Dame head coach Tyrone Willingham previews this weekend's game at USC. Willingham discusses the BCS rankings, walk-ons, the Trojans and more in this week's press conference.

NEWS AND NOTES

• Football Central
• Golden Moments In Irish Football History
• Game Notes
• Depth Chart
• Updated Bios
• 2002 Schedule
• 2002 Roster
• 2002 Statistics
• 2002 Statistics
• 2001 Results
• Future Schedules
• Multimedia
• Strength & Conditioning Info!

HEAD COACH
• Tyrone Willingham

Internet

▲ *Notre Dame still has one of the premier programs in college football.*

His locker-room speeches became legendary. In honor of George Gipp, a Notre Dame star who had recently died, Rockne asked his team to "Win one for the Gipper!" They did, again and again.

Rockne's victories, speeches, newspaper columns, and product endorsements made him one of the most well-known men in the country. When he died in a 1931 plane crash, the nation mourned. In the seven decades since Rockne's death, no coach has come close to passing his winning percentage of .881.

John Dillinger

The Federal Bureau of Investigation (FBI) called John Dillinger "Public Enemy Number One." During the 1930s, he was the most famous bank robber in the nation.

Dillinger was born in 1903. He grew up on a farm in Mooresville, Indiana. When he was twenty, he was imprisoned for beating up a man. During his nine years in prison, he was surrounded by hardened criminals who taught him how to rob banks.

When he was released, Dillinger organized a violent gang. Soon they were America's most successful and notorious bank robbers. They killed fifteen people as they stole a total of $300,000 from eleven banks.

In 1934, Dillinger was captured, but, using a wooden gun, he tricked his guards and escaped. A few months later, police tracked him to a lodge in Wisconsin. When they attempted to arrest him, Dillinger started shooting. Three bystanders were killed, and the gangster once again escaped.

Authorities, especially FBI officials, were embarrassed that they could not get their hands on "Public Enemy Number One." After a massive manhunt, agents finally cornered him outside a Chicago theater on July 22, 1934. When he pulled a gun, he was shot and killed.

James Dean

Born in Marion, Indiana, James Byron Dean took the movie industry by storm. Although he only appeared in three films, he quickly became an American legend. His most famous role was as a troubled youth in *Rebel Without a Cause,* released in 1955. People still collect photos of him, nearly fifty years after his death.

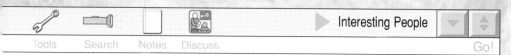
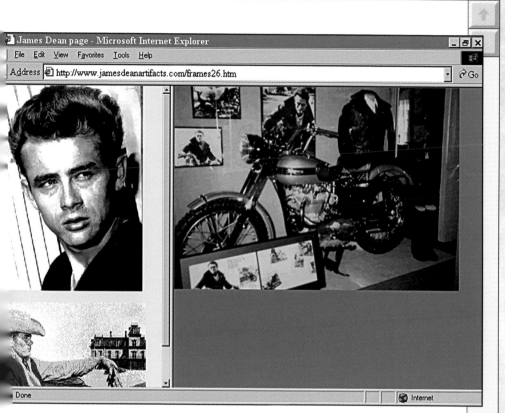

▲ *Born and raised in Indiana, actor James Dean was killed in a motorcycle accident on September 30, 1955, at the age of twenty-four. He remains a Hollywood legend to this day.*

▶ Michael Jackson

During the 1980s, the most popular and successful recording artist in the world was Michael Jackson. When he was just four years old in Gary, Indiana, his father organized him and his older brothers into a musical group known as the Jackson Five. Soon the talented youngster was the lead singer. Before Michael was a teenager, the group had number one hits such as "I Want You Back" and "I'll Be There."

In 1979, when he was twenty-one, he released a solo album, *Off the Wall,* which became a big hit. Two years later, *Thriller* became the best-selling album in history. Catchy, exciting songs, such as "Beat It" and "Billie Jean," and Jackson's incredible dancing made him MTV's biggest star.

In 2001, Jackson celebrated thirty years as a solo performer with a spectacular concert in New York City and the release of *Invincible,* his first new album in six years.

▶ Twyla Tharp

When she was a young girl growing up in Portland, Indiana, Twyla Tharp loved to dance. She thought about making a career out of her talent but was afraid there were very few jobs. "Too bad," she finally decided. "This is what I do best, and this is what I'm going to do."[2]

Tharp need not have worried. She became a successful modern dancer and choreographed dances of her own. Many of them were performed by the superstar dancer Mikhail Baryshnikov.

Tharp choreographed the movies *Hair, Amadeus, Ragtime,* and *White Nights* and the Broadway play *Singin' in the Rain.*

In 1992, she published her autobiography, *Push Comes to Shove.* Tharp continues to design new pieces and organize performing tours across the country.

▶ Bobby Knight

When Bobby Knight became head men's basketball coach at Indiana University in 1971, few people had heard of him. Twenty-nine years later, after eleven Big Ten Conference titles and three national championships, his was a household name.

Despite his success at winning games and encouraging his players to remain in college and graduate, Knight was best known for his temper. He threw a chair onto the court, allegedly choked and kicked players, stuffed a man into a garbage can at a bar, cursed at reporters, and was arrested for assaulting a policeman in Puerto Rico.

University officials finally ran out of patience with Knight. He was fired in 2000. Six months later, he was hired as the head basketball coach at Texas Tech University.

▶ Ryan White

On December 26, 1984, Ryan White received terrible news. He had AIDS, then a new disease. Ryan was only thirteen years old, but he had never been healthy. He had hemophilia, a disease that prevents the blood from clotting properly. A blood transfusion treatment for that disease had accidentally given him AIDS.

At that time, not much was known about the new disease except that it seemed to kill all its victims. Many people worried that it could be spread by casual contact like sharing a drinking fountain or by someone sneezing.

Ryan's schoolmates in Kokomo, Indiana, were scared. They did not want to sit next to him or share drinking fountains and cafeteria silverware. They called him names and vandalized his locker. Finally, the school ordered him to stay home.[3]

▲ *Ryan White became the poster child for the fight against AIDS during the 1980s and 1990s.*

Ryan and his mother sued and finally won back his right to attend school. Celebrities such as Michael Jackson, Elizabeth Taylor, and Elton John came to his defense. Thanks to Ryan and the doctors who spoke out for him, Americans learned that AIDS could not be spread by casual contact. Articles and books were written about Ryan's struggle. *The Ryan White Story* was a popular television movie. In 1990, the brave young man succumbed to AIDS when he was just eighteen.

▷ Jane Pauley

Very few anchors have appeared on television as long—or as often—as Jane Pauley. She began her career at WISH-TV in her hometown of Indianapolis shortly after graduating from Indiana University. She was only twenty-five when she became coanchor of *The Today Show* in 1976. For thirteen years, she worked with Tom Brokaw and Bryant Gumbel.

After leaving the show, she moved on to other programs such as *Real Life With Jane Pauley* and *Dateline NBC*, the only major network magazine program that appeared five times a week. As a journalist for almost thirty years, she has won numerous awards in her career. In 1998, she was inducted into the Broadcasting and Cable Hall of Fame.

▷ David Letterman

David Letterman, too, might have become a television journalist, but his sense of humor got in the way. He grew up in Indianapolis and attended Ball State University in Muncie. After graduating, he hosted a children's program and late-night movies. He also worked as a news anchor and weatherman. His bosses expected him to be serious on the air, but he could not help telling jokes.

Soon he was writing television comedy shows in Los Angeles. By 1980, he had his own morning network talk show on NBC-TV. That led to a popular late night show that lasted a dozen years on the same network.

In 1993, Letterman moved to CBS-TV, where his show continued to be especially popular with young adults. In 2002, television executives attempted to lure him to ABC-TV with a multimillion dollar offer. Instead he chose to remain at CBS.

Letterman is best known for his cynical sense of humor, comedy bits like "Stupid Pet Tricks," and his top ten lists.

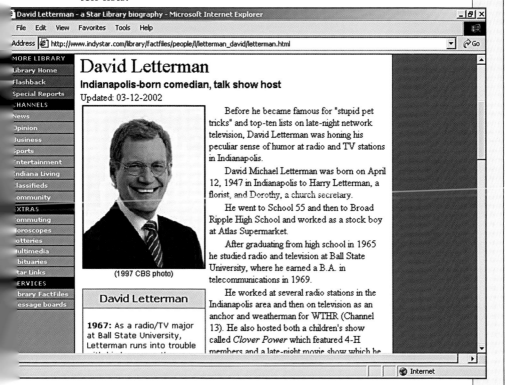

David Letterman - a Star Library biography - Microsoft Internet Explorer

File   Edit   View   Favorites   Tools   Help

Address   http://www.indystar.com/library/factfiles/people/l/letterman_david/letterman.html   Go

MORE LIBRARY
Library Home
Flashback
Special Reports
CHANNELS
News
Opinion
Business
Sports
Entertainment
Indiana Living
Classifieds
Community
EXTRAS
Commuting
Horoscopes
Lotteries
Multimedia
Obituaries
Star Links
SERVICES
Library FactFiles
Message boards

David Letterman
Indianapolis-born comedian, talk show host
Updated: 03-12-2002

David Letterman

1967: As a radio/TV major at Ball State University, Letterman runs into trouble

(1997 CBS photo)

Before he became famous for "stupid pet tricks" and top-ten lists on late-night network television, David Letterman was honing his peculiar sense of humor at radio and TV stations in Indianapolis.

David Michael Letterman was born on April 12, 1947 in Indianapolis to Harry Letterman, a florist, and Dorothy, a church secretary.

He went to School 55 and then to Broad Ripple High School and worked as a stock boy at Atlas Supermarket.

After graduating from high school in 1965 he studied radio and television at Ball State University, where he earned a B.A. in telecommunications in 1969.

He worked at several radio stations in the Indianapolis area and then on television as an anchor and weatherman for WTHR (Channel 13). He also hosted both a children's show called *Clover Power* which featured 4-H members and a late-night movie show which he

Internet

Born in Indianapolis, Indiana, David Letterman has become a very popular television host.

Chapter 4 ▶

The Government, Economy, and Cities

Like other states, Indiana's state government is divided into three branches—executive, legislative, and judicial. The governor heads the executive branch. It is a powerful job. He or she appoints many important government officials and sets their salaries. Like the lieutenant governor, attorney general, secretary of state, auditor, and treasurer, the governor is elected to a four-year term.

▲ *The Corydon Capitol (shown here), located in Corydon, Indiana, was the state's capitol building from 1813 to 1825. Today, the new capitol building is in Indianapolis.*

▲ *Although farmland covers almost 70 percent of Indiana, most Hoosiers work in the manufacturing industry.*

▶ Running the State

Indiana's legislative branch has two parts—the one hundred-member house of representatives and fifty-member senate. Those two bodies make the state's laws. The state constitution limits them to short sessions of no more than sixty-one days a year.

A chief justice and four associate justices make up Indiana's supreme court. There is also a court of appeals with fifteen judges and various circuit and county courts.

The state raises most of its money by a sales tax and an income tax.

▶ Making Money

Indiana's eighty thousand farms cover almost 70 percent of the state's land. The most important crops are corn and soybeans. No other state grows more corn used to make

popcorn than Indiana. Tomatoes and apples from Indiana are also marketed throughout the United States. The most important livestock product is hogs.

However, most Hoosiers are not employed in farming. They work for businesses that manufacture products. Indiana factories make chemicals, electrical products, steel, and transportation equipment. Many workers are involved in service industries such as government work, health care, tourism, and retail stores.

Hoosiers

There are few American Indians left in the "Land of the Indian." Most of them lost their homes to the early white settlers.

Indiana never allowed slavery, so there were very few African Americans in the state until after the Civil War. In the early twentieth century, African Americans came north to take factory jobs. According to the 2000 census, only 8.4 percent of Hoosiers are African American.

Most of Indiana's population are Caucasian descendents of European immigrants from Germany, Great Britain, France, Ireland, and the Netherlands.

Cities

Most Hoosiers live in urban areas. The biggest city is Indianapolis, with 791,926 people as of 2000.[1] Since 1825, it has been the state capital. It is probably best known for the Indianapolis 500 auto race, although it is also the home of two professional sports teams—basketball's Indiana Pacers and football's Indianapolis Colts.

The homes of two of Indiana's most famous citizens— President Benjamin Harrison and James Whitcomb Riley—are preserved there as museums. Visitors also enjoy

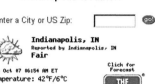

▲ *Indianapolis is the capital of Indiana. It is also the most populous city in the state.*

the Indianapolis Museum of Art, the Indiana State Museum, and the Children's Museum.

Indianapolis and Marion County merged in 1970. The merger simplified local government and made Indianapolis one of the country's largest cities.

Fort Wayne, Indiana's second largest city with 205,727 residents, hosts a Three Rivers Festival every summer. Thousands enjoy parades, foods, and tributes to state history.

The city actually got its start when a fort was built there in 1794 by General "Mad" Anthony Wayne. Fort Wayne's downtown area got a makeover in the 1980s when

a botanical garden, convention center, and art museum were built.

Evansville sits on the banks of the Ohio River. Its population reached one hundred thousand in 2000. The Museum of Arts and Sciences is located in the downtown area. The Angel Mounds, built by the ancient Mound Builders, also draws visitors.

During the 1980s, when thousands of factory jobs disappeared, Gary, Indiana, lost a fourth of its population. However, by 2000, it was still Indiana's fourth largest city with a population of 102,746. It also is still one of the nation's most important steel producers. Despite its heavy industry, in the last thirty years the city and its factories have successfully worked together to reduce air pollution.

History

For almost two centuries, the people of Indiana have called themselves Hoosiers. It is now the nickname of the Indiana University athletic teams.

"What exactly is a Hoosier?" one may ask. Is it an animal, a plant, an American Indian name? Despite decades of research, nobody knows. All that is known for sure is

Angel Mounds State Historic Site - Microsoft Internet Explorer

File Edit View Favorites Tools Help

Address http://www.angelmounds.org/

Home
Welcome
History
Events
Exhibits
Friends
Directions
Kids Corner
Links
Other Sites
Announcements
Gift Shop

Make an online
donation to
Angel Mounds.

PayPal
DONATE

You are visitor
number 25353 since
November 4, 2000

Angel Mounds
State Historic Site

May 23, 2002 - The Angel Mounds New Land Purchase Photos are online. There are also photos of the Mound A Stabilization Project Online.

Internet

▲ Angel Mounds, located on the northern bank of the Ohio River in Evansville, Indiana, was perhaps the largest settlement of its time period. It was inhabited by American Indians from approximately A.D.1100 to A.D.1450 when, for unknown reasons, they abandoned the location.

that by the 1830s, the word was used and recognized as a nickname for the people of Indiana.[1]

Land of the Indian

We can be sure, however, about the meaning of the name Indiana itself. Take off the "a" and it is easy to see. The name of the state means "Land of the Indian," as in American Indians. Throughout most of its history, that is exactly what Indiana was.

The first residents of the region that would eventually be called Indiana were American Indians now known as Mound Builders. They built villages and constructed burial mounds.

When the first European settlers arrived, the only American Indians in Indiana were the Miami. This changed as more and more European settlers arrived in the East, pushing other American Indian tribes into Indiana. The Delaware, Munsee, and Shawnee made new homes as did the Potawatomi.

The French

René Robert Cavelier, also known as Sieur de La Salle, was a French explorer. He was probably the first European in Indiana. He was there in 1679, looking for a water route to the Pacific Ocean. LaSalle was followed by many French fur traders.

After the French and Indian War, the French gave Indiana and other territory to the British in 1763. During the American Revolution, colonial General George Rogers Clark occupied Fort Sackwell, a British fort near Vincennes. After the war, Indiana became part of America's Northwest Territory.

American Indian Resistance

As settlers poured into the area, some were attacked by angry Miami Indians led by Chief Little Turtle. The chief and his followers were defeated by General "Mad" Anthony Wayne.

Tecumseh, a Shawnee chief, organized several tribes into a powerful force to battle the Americans. They were defeated by General William Henry Harrison, Indiana Territory's first governor, in the Battle of Tippecanoe.

Gradually, the tribes were moved even farther west. The last American Indians left were a few Potawatomi in the northern part of the state. However, almost all of them were driven out in 1838. There were then almost no American Indians left in the Land of the Indian.

Inventions and Construction

Indiana became a state in 1816. It grew quickly because of the new National Road that stretched across the state from Cumberland, Maryland, to Vandalia, Illinois. The road, which was really just a

The Tippecanoe Battlefield Memorial, located in Battle Ground, Indiana, marks the spot where General William Henry Harrison defeated Tecumseh.

43

cleared wagon path, carried thousands of new settlers from the East. It was the first of many roads to make Indianapolis one of America's important crossroads.

Railroads, which arrived in the 1850s, made travel even easier. In 1886, the Standard Oil Company began drilling for oil near Lake Michigan. The biggest oil refinery in the world was built in Whiting. Gary, Indiana, became the site of a giant steel plant in 1906. Many glass-making factories were constructed in Muncie and around the state. Gilbert Van Camp opened a canning company in Indianapolis that sent pork and beans and other foods across the country.

One of the first automobiles was designed and built in Kokomo, Indiana, by Elwood Haynes in 1894. He was the first manufacturer to sell cars with electrical starting

▲ *The Turner Doll factory, located in Bedford, Indiana, allows visitors to see the art of doll making.*

systems and clutches. The Studebaker brothers, Clement and John, began assembling cars in South Bend in 1904.

Because of its central location, Indiana was crisscrossed in the 1950s by important federal highways. All the construction has made the state's road map look like an octopus. Indianapolis sits in the middle with interstate highways radiating out in seven directions. Across the top of the state, the Indiana Toll Road was opened in 1956.

Many factories were built in the larger cities. Indianapolis and Gary became important industrial centers. The cities grew even larger as thousands of workers flocked to new jobs. The factories were a steady source of jobs until the Great Depression of the 1930s. By the end of World War II, most factories were operating successfully again.

In the 1970s, the state economy was strengthened by the success of the Port of Indiana in Burns Harbor, on Lake Michigan. Then, economic problems in the 1980s forced many of the factories near the cities to close. In addition, farmers were having trouble getting decent prices for their goods. By the 1990s, though, the state began redevelopment projects in the cities, with hopes that they would spur the economy.

Indiana Facts

1. Official description from Indiana Code 1-2-2-1, quoted in, *USA State Symbols, Flags and Facts,* CD-ROM, Canada: Robesus, Inc., 2001.

Chapter 1. Crossroads of America

1. Don Markstein, "Garfield," *Don Markstein's Toonopedia,* 2000, <http://www.toonopedia.com/garfield .htm> (October 17, 2002).

Chapter 3. Interesting Hoosiers

1. Crystal Reference, "Debs, Eugene V. (Victor)," *Biography.com,* 2001, <http://search.biography.com/print_ record.pl?id=14128> (October 17, 2002).

2. Jordan Levin, "Still Getting Her Kicks," *Dance90210.com* (reprinted from the Los Angeles Times), n.d., <http://www.dance90210.com/interview.html> (November 8, 2002).

3. Bill Shaw, "Candle in the Wind," *People Magazine,* April 23, 1990, vol. 33, pp. 86–90.

Chapter 4. The Government, Economy, and Cities

1. All population data is according to the 2000 U.S. Census, as recorded in the *Time Almanac 2002* (Boston: Information Please, 2001), p. 149.

Chapter 5. History

1. *The American Heritage Dictionary of the English Language,* fourth edition, as appears on "Hoosiers," *Bartleby.com,* 2000, <http://www.bartleby.com/61/16/ H0271600.html> (October 17, 2002).

Further Reading

Aretha, David. *The Notre Dame Fighting Irish Football Team.* Berkeley Heights, N.J.: Enslow Publishers, Inc., 2001.

Boekhoff, P. M. and Stuart A. Kallen. *Indiana.* Farmington Hills, Mich.: Gale Group, 2001.

Brill, Marlene T. *Indiana.* Tarrytown, N.Y.: Marshall Cavendish, 1997.

Brunelle, Lynn. *Indiana: The Hoosier State.* Milwaukee: Gareth Stevens Incorporated, 2002.

Craats, Rennay. *A Guide to Indiana.* Mankato, Minn.: Weigl Publishers, Inc., 2001.

Fradin, Dennis Brill. *Indiana.* Danbury, Conn.: Children's Press, 1997.

Heinrichs, Ann. *Indiana. America the Beautiful.* Danbury, Conn.: Children's Press, 2000.

Kavanagh, James. *Indiana Birds.* Blaine, Wash.: Waterford Press, 1999.

McAuliffe, Bill. *Indiana Facts & Symbols.* Minnetonka, Minn.: Capstone Press, Inc., 1999.

Swain, Gwenyth. *Indiana: Hello U.S.A.* Minneapolis, Minn.: Lerner Publishing Group, 2002.

Thompson, Kathleen. *Indiana.* Austin, Tex.: Raintree Steck-Vaughn Publishers, 1996.

A
American Indians, 23, 38, 41–43
Amish Acres, 24
Angel Mounds, 40–41
area, 11

B
Ball State University, 34

C
Cavelier, René Robert, 42
climate, 21
composers, 17
Corydon Capitol, 36
covered bridges, 24–25

D
Davis, Jim, 16
Dean, James, 30–31
Debs, Eugene V., 27–28
Dillinger, John, 30

E
economy
    agriculture, 37–38
    manufacturing, 37–38, 40, 44, 44–45
    service industries, 38
Evansville, Indiana, 40

F
Fort Wayne, Indiana, 24, 39–40

G
Gary, Indiana, 22, 31, 40, 45
geography
    Great Lakes Plains, 18, 20
    Lake Michigan, 21–22, 44–45
    Southern Hills and Lowlands, 20
    Till Plains, 20
    Wyandotte Cave, 24
government, state, 36–37
Great Depression, 45

H
Harrison, Benjamin, 26, 38
Harrison, William Henry, 23–24, 26, 43
high school sports teams
    Martinsville High School, 13
    Milan Indians, 14–15
    Muncie Central, 15
highways, 11, 24, 43, 45

L
Letterman, David, 34–35

I
Indiana Dunes National Lakeshore, 22
Indiana University, 13–14, 32–34, 41
Indianapolis, Indiana, 16, 34–35,
        38–39, 45
Indianapolis 500, 11–12, 38–39
Indianapolis Motor Speedway, 11–12, 24

J
Jackson, Michael, 31–32, 34

K
Knight, Bobby, 32–33
Kokomo, Indiana, 33, 44

L
limestone, 21, 24
Lincoln, Abraham, 22–23
Lincoln Boyhood National
        Memorial, 22–23

N
National Road, 24, 43–44

P
Pauley, Jane, 34
population, 11, 38–40
professional sports teams
        Indiana Pacers, 13–14, 38
        Indianapolis Colts, 38
Purdue College, 13
Pyle, Ernie, 15–16

R
Riley, James Whitcomb, 15, 38
Rockne, Knute, 13, 28–29

S
South Bend, Indiana, 12, 45

T
Tharp, Twyla, 32
Tippecanoe Battlefield and Museum,
        23, 43

U
University of Notre Dame, 12–13, 28–29

W
Wayne, General "Mad" Anthony, 24,
        39, 43
White, Ryan, 33–34
wildlife, 23, 25
William Henry Harrison Home, 23